I0482548

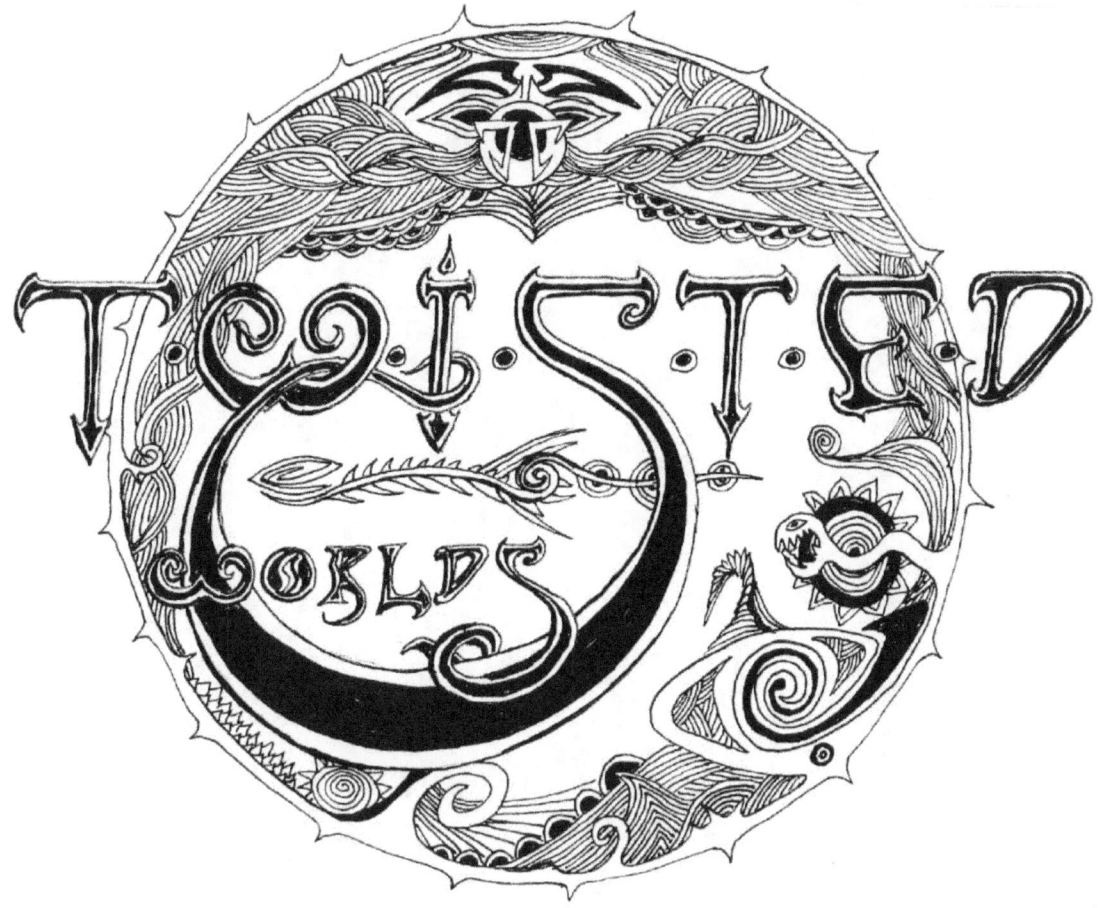

Joe Cowin brings to you some of his magnificent creations in this series called Twisted.

Joe Cowin is a creative artist who has been drawing since he was a child and whose works are found hanging on various walls around England and New Zealand.

When taking time away from being a Nurse, Joe likes to travel and be inspired by his surroundings, with a particular interest in macabre and fantasy.

[f] Check us out on Facebook – Adult Colouring by Joe Cowin

We hope you Enjoy!!!!

This edition published in 2016 by Amazon Books

Copyright © Joe Cowin

All rights reserved. No part of this publication may be reproduced, stored in a retrieval system, or transmitted, in any form or by any means, electronic, mechanical, photocopying, recording or otherwise, without prior written permission in accordance with the provisions of the Copyright Act 1956 (as amended). Any person or persons who do any unauthorised act in relation to this publication may be liable to criminal prosecution and civil claims for damages.

ISBN-13: 978-153496600
ISBN-10: 1534966005

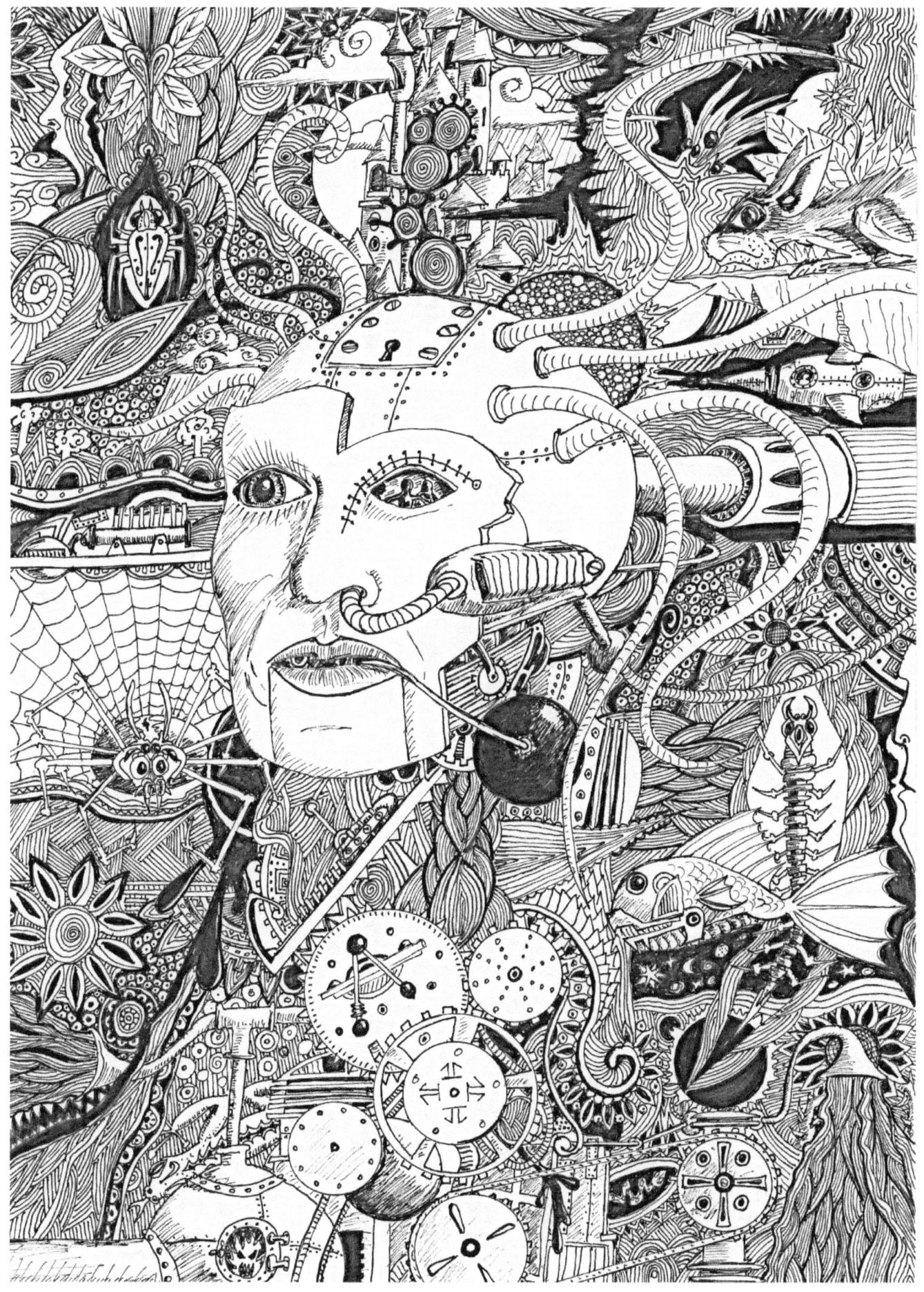

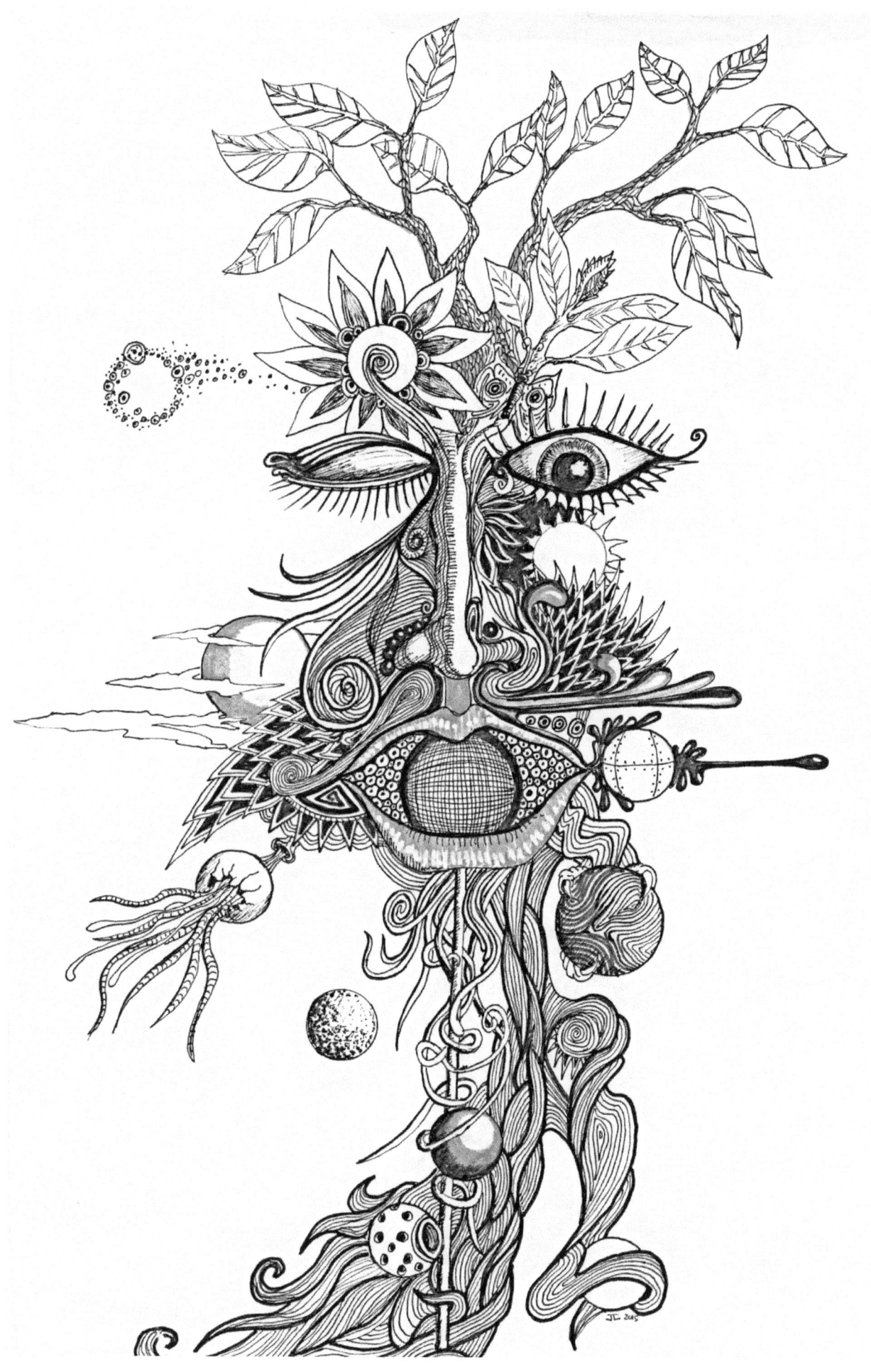

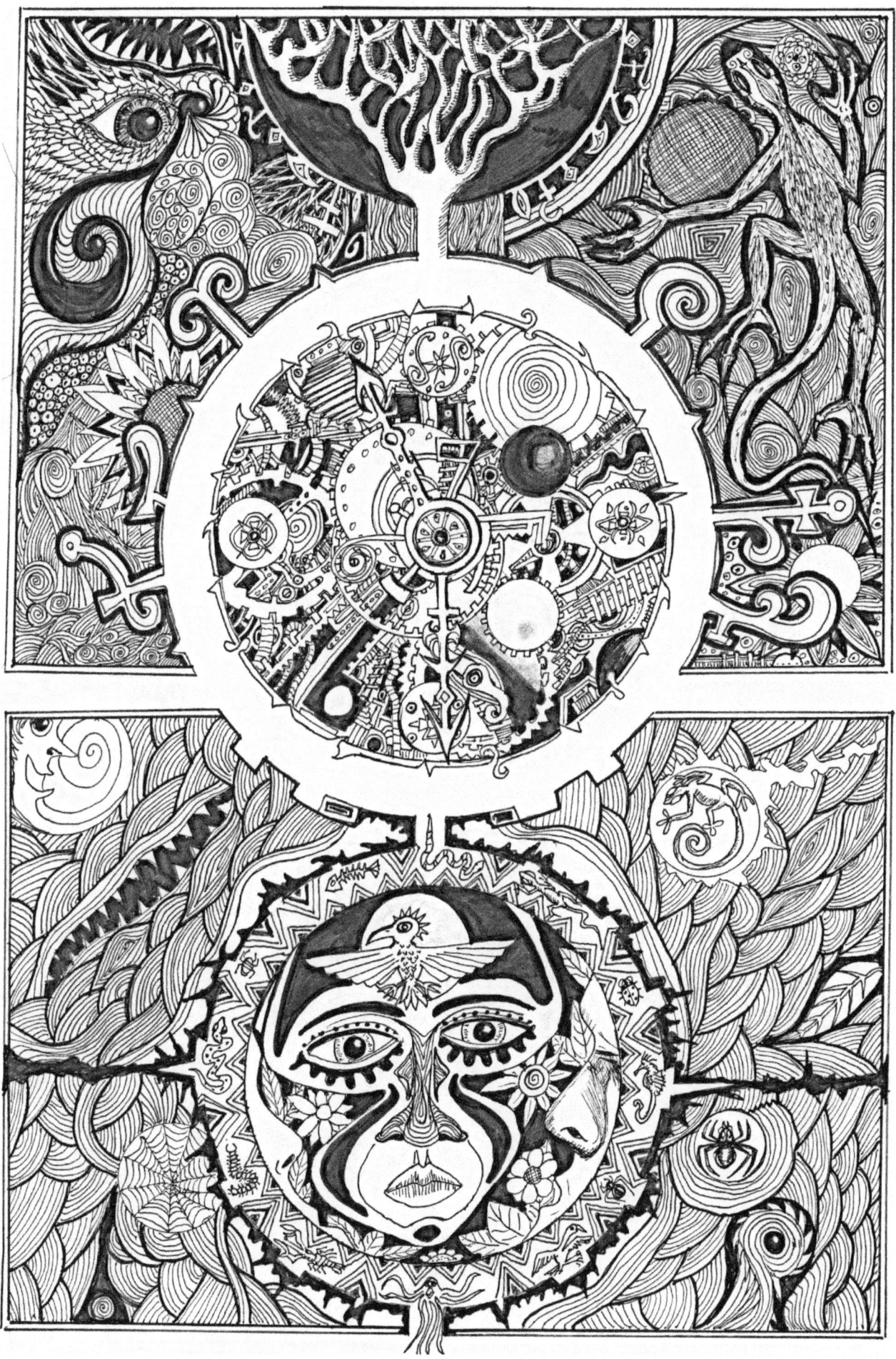

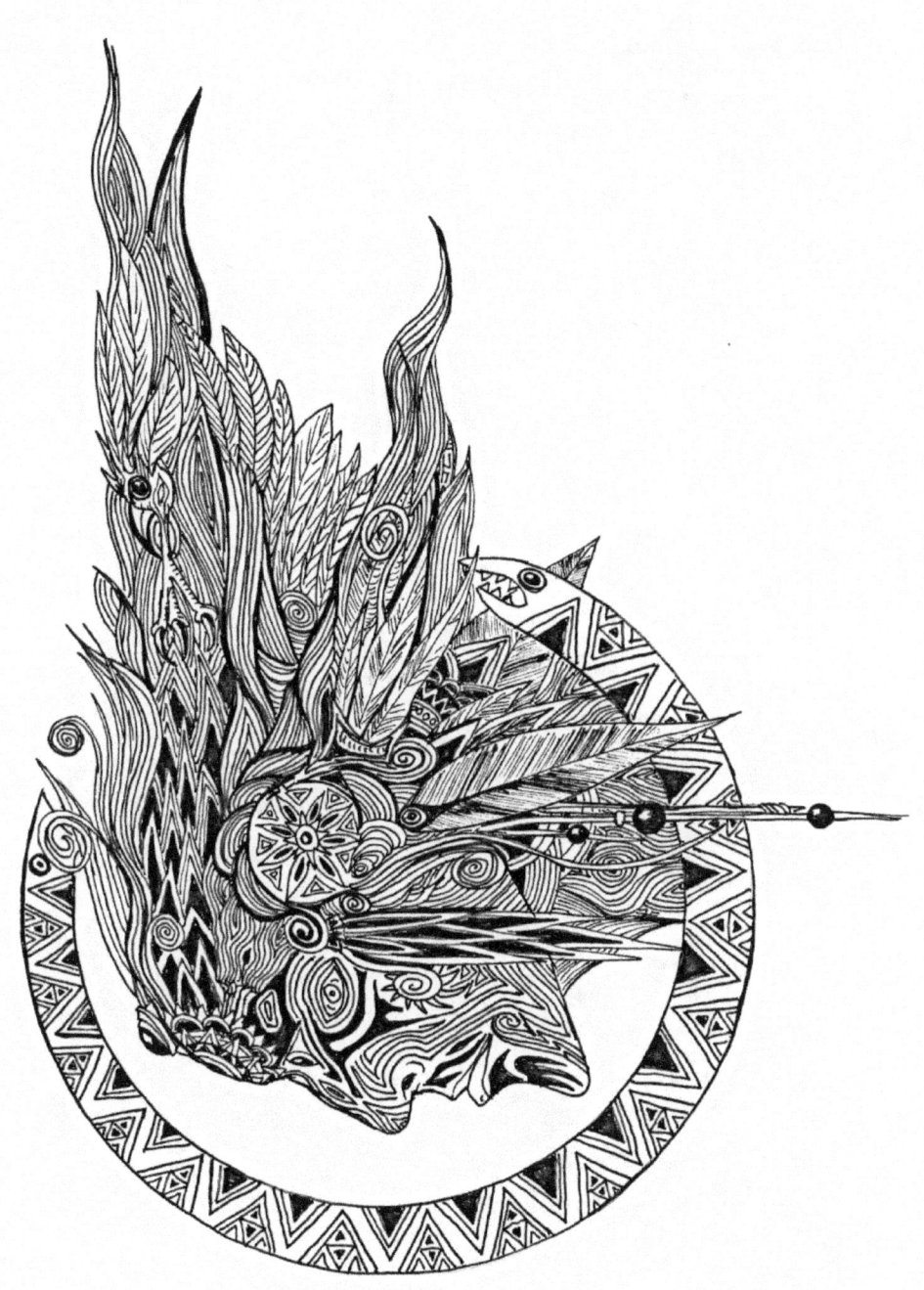

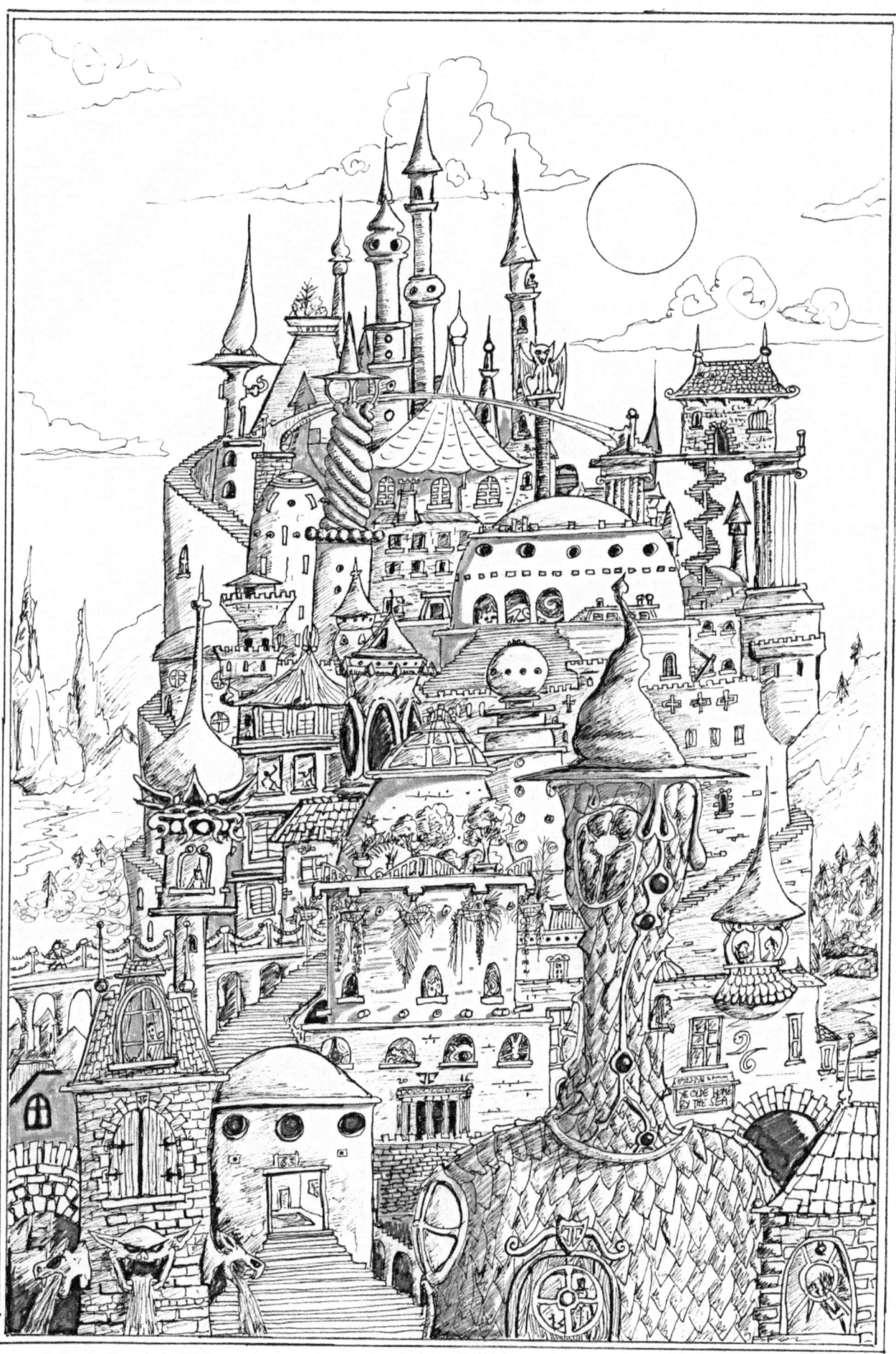

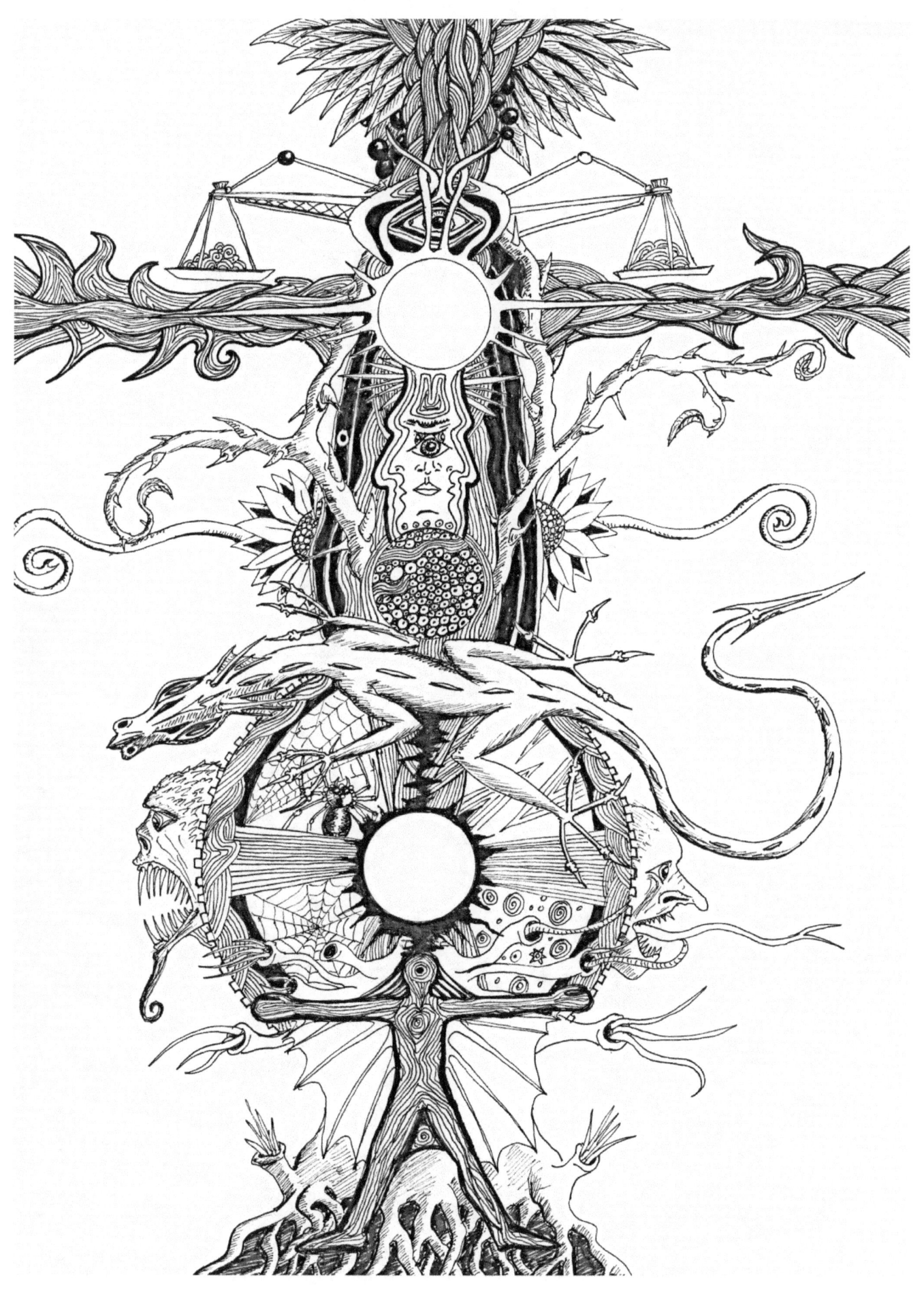

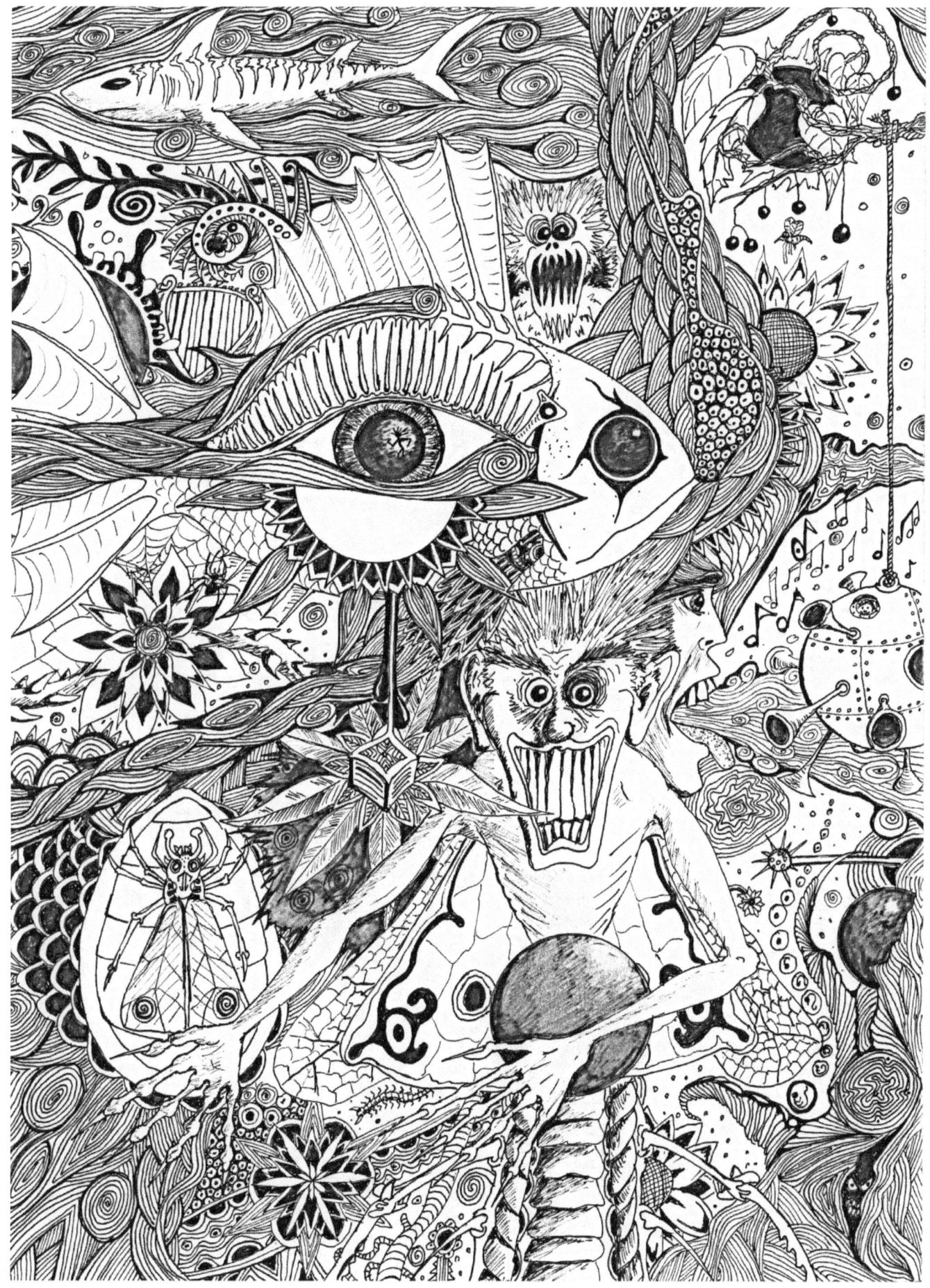

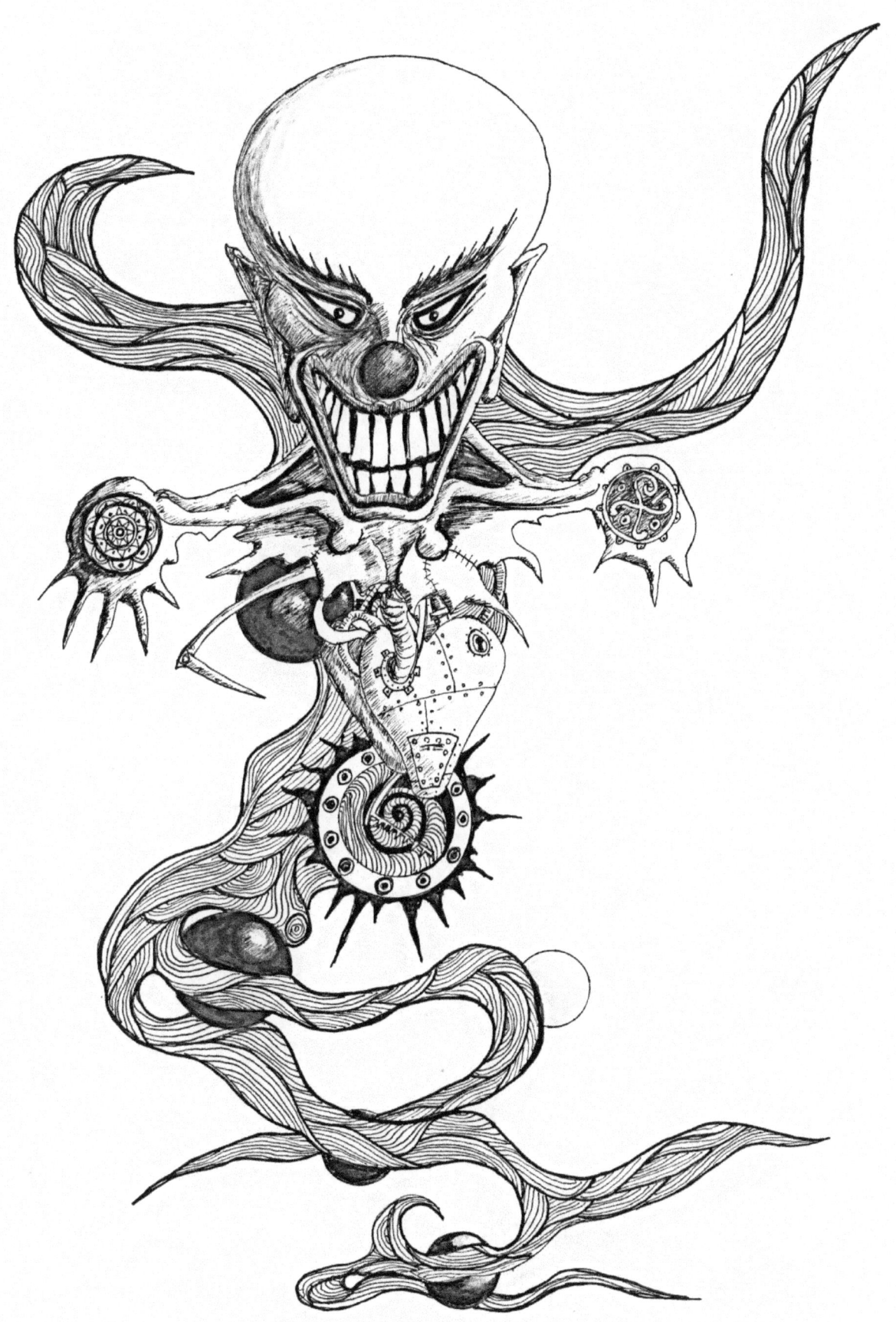

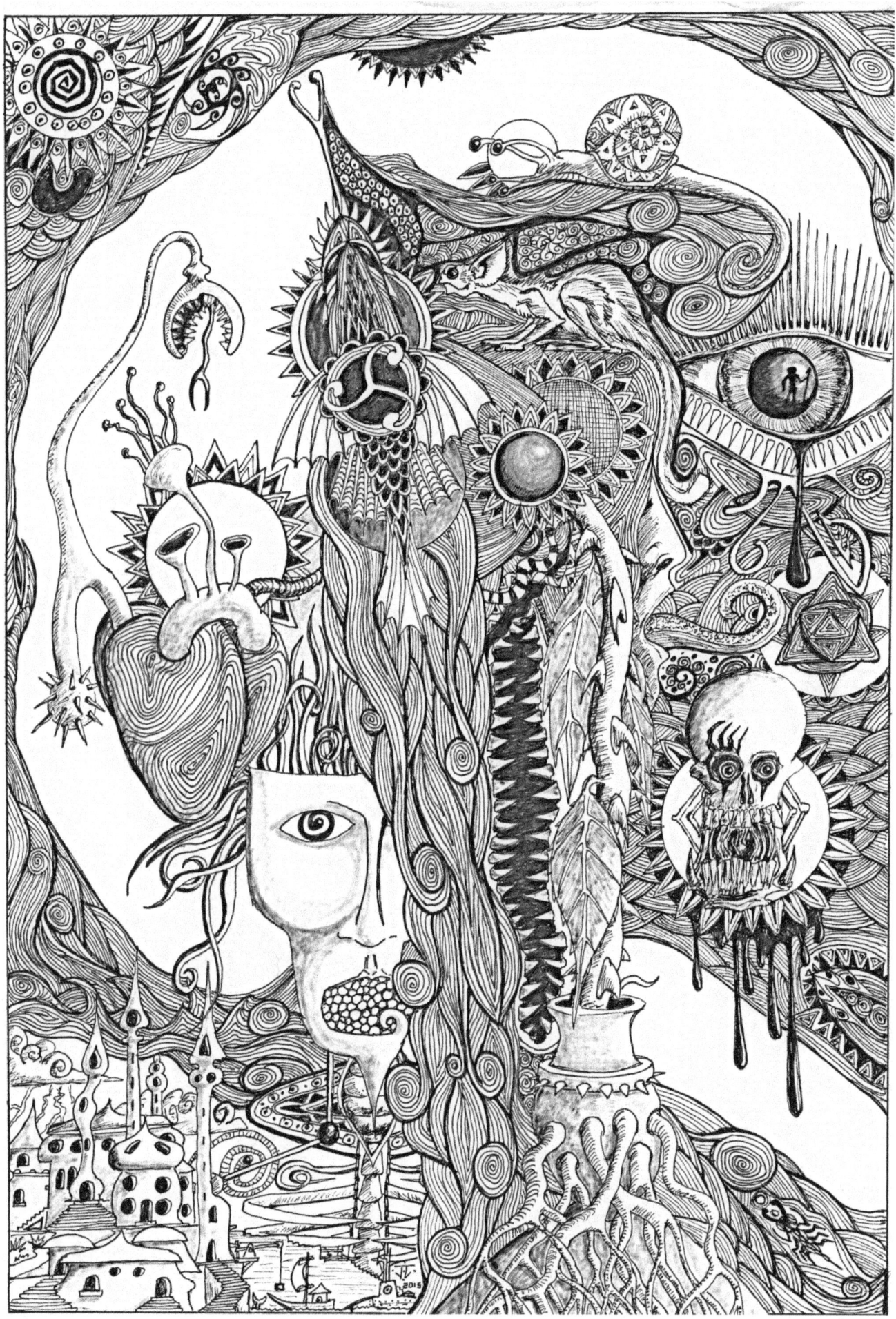

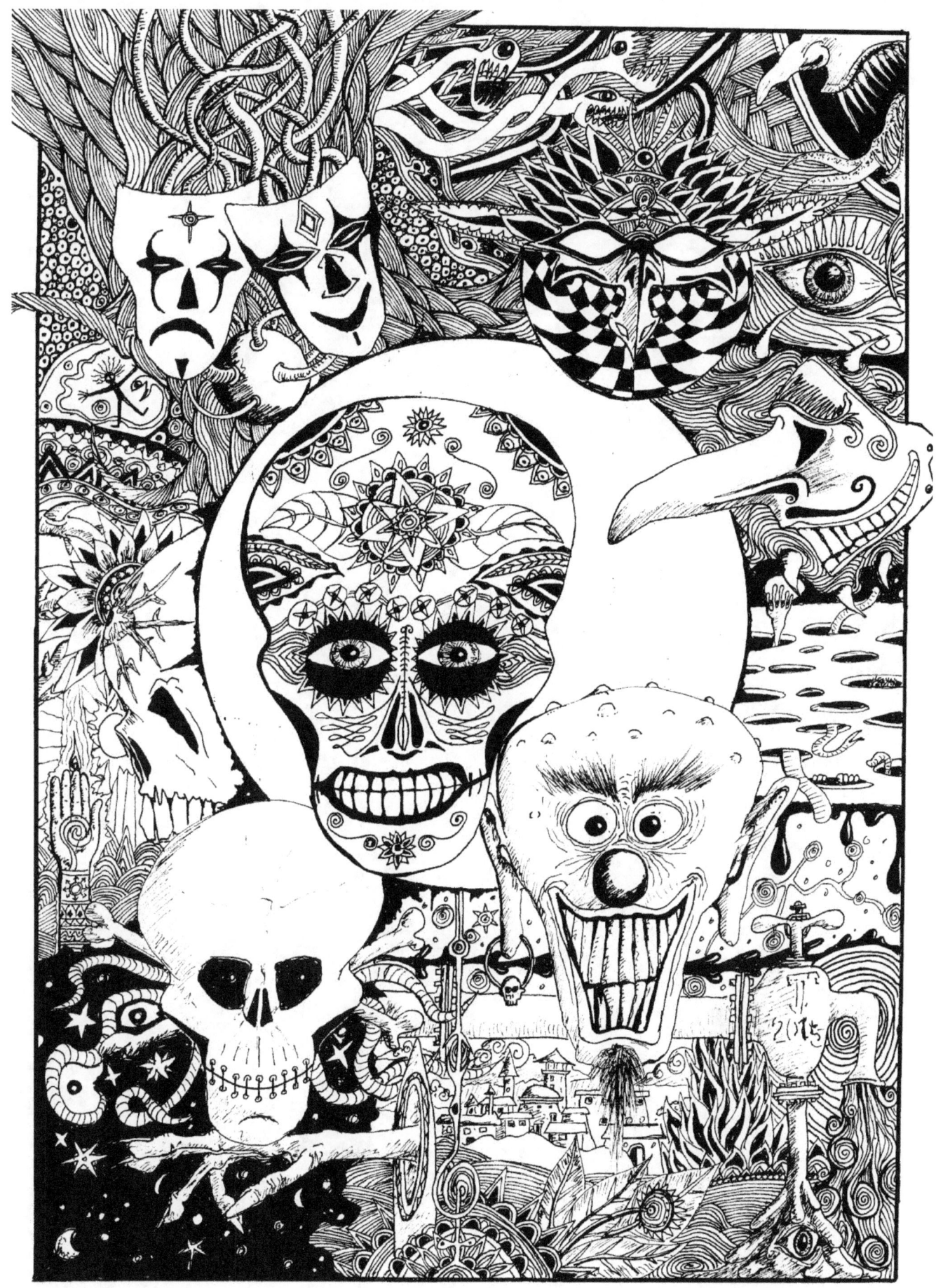

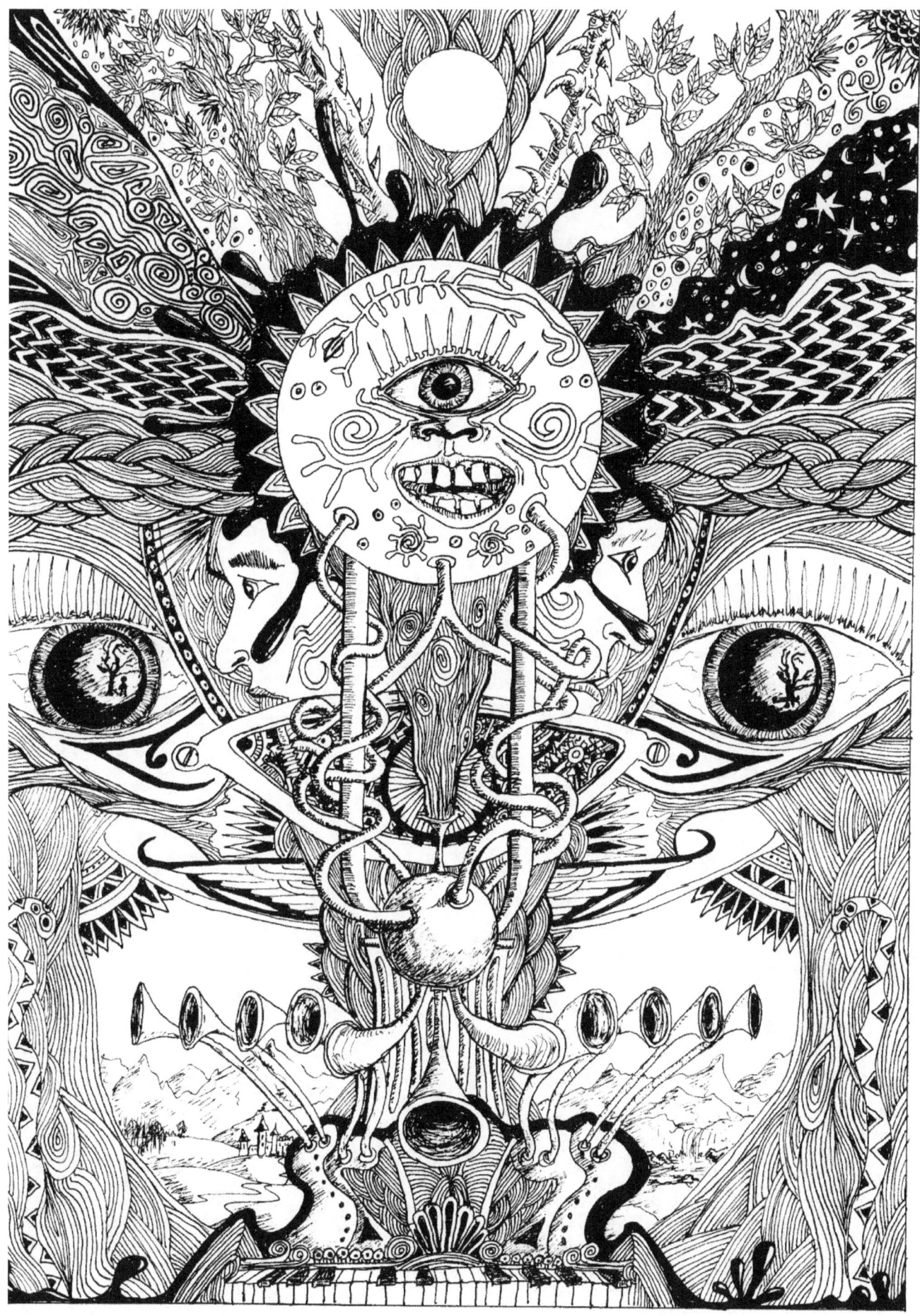

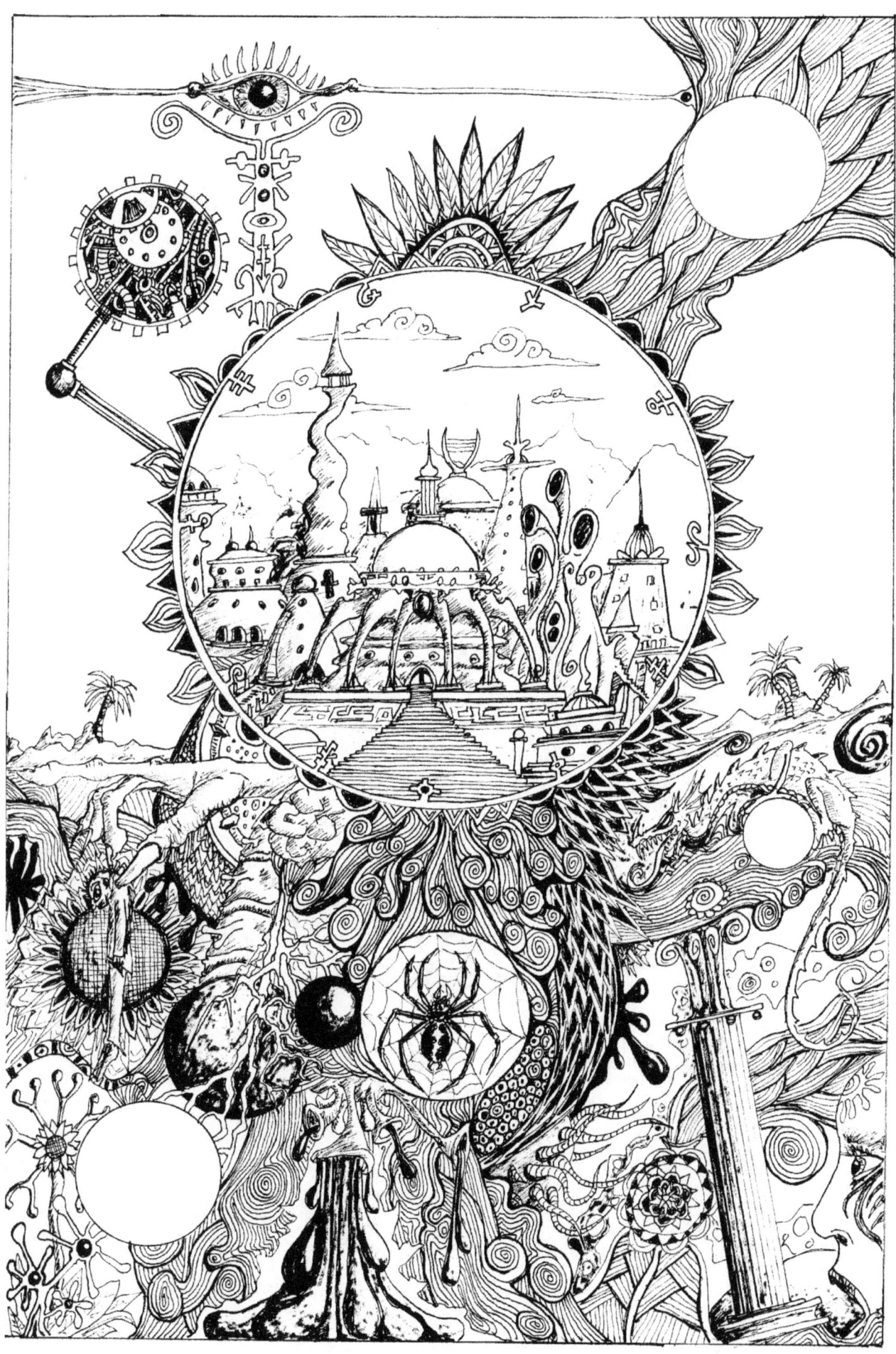

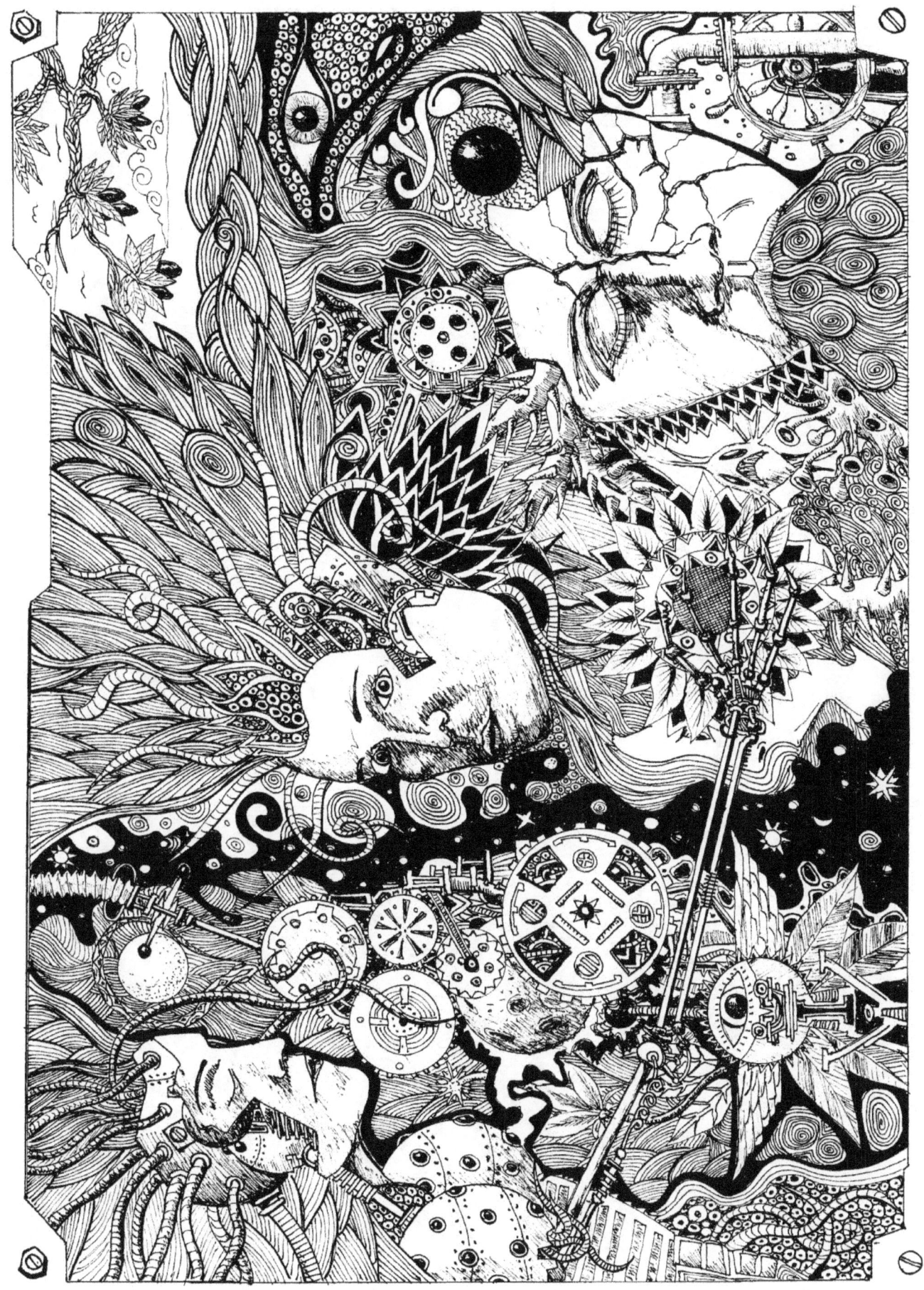

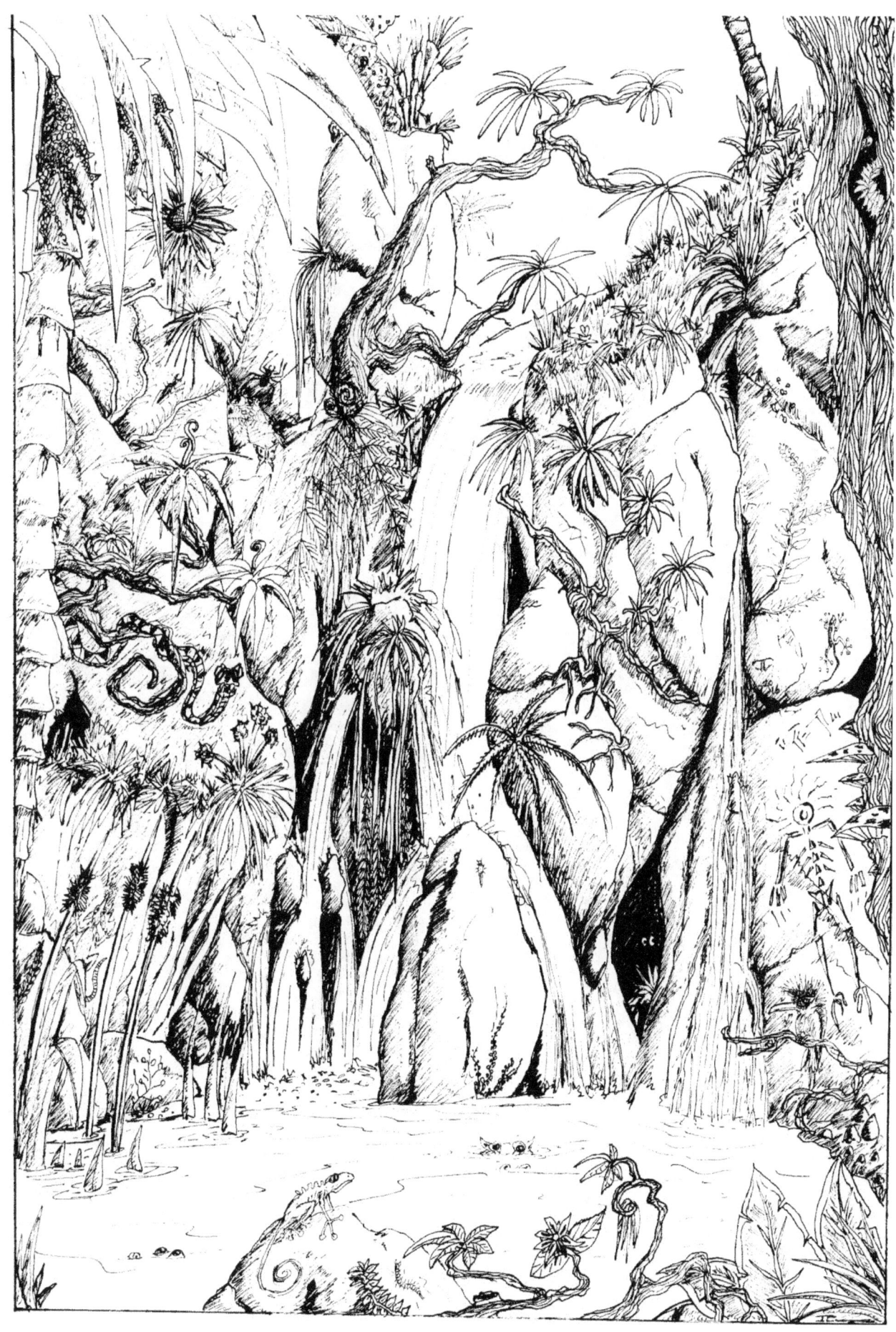

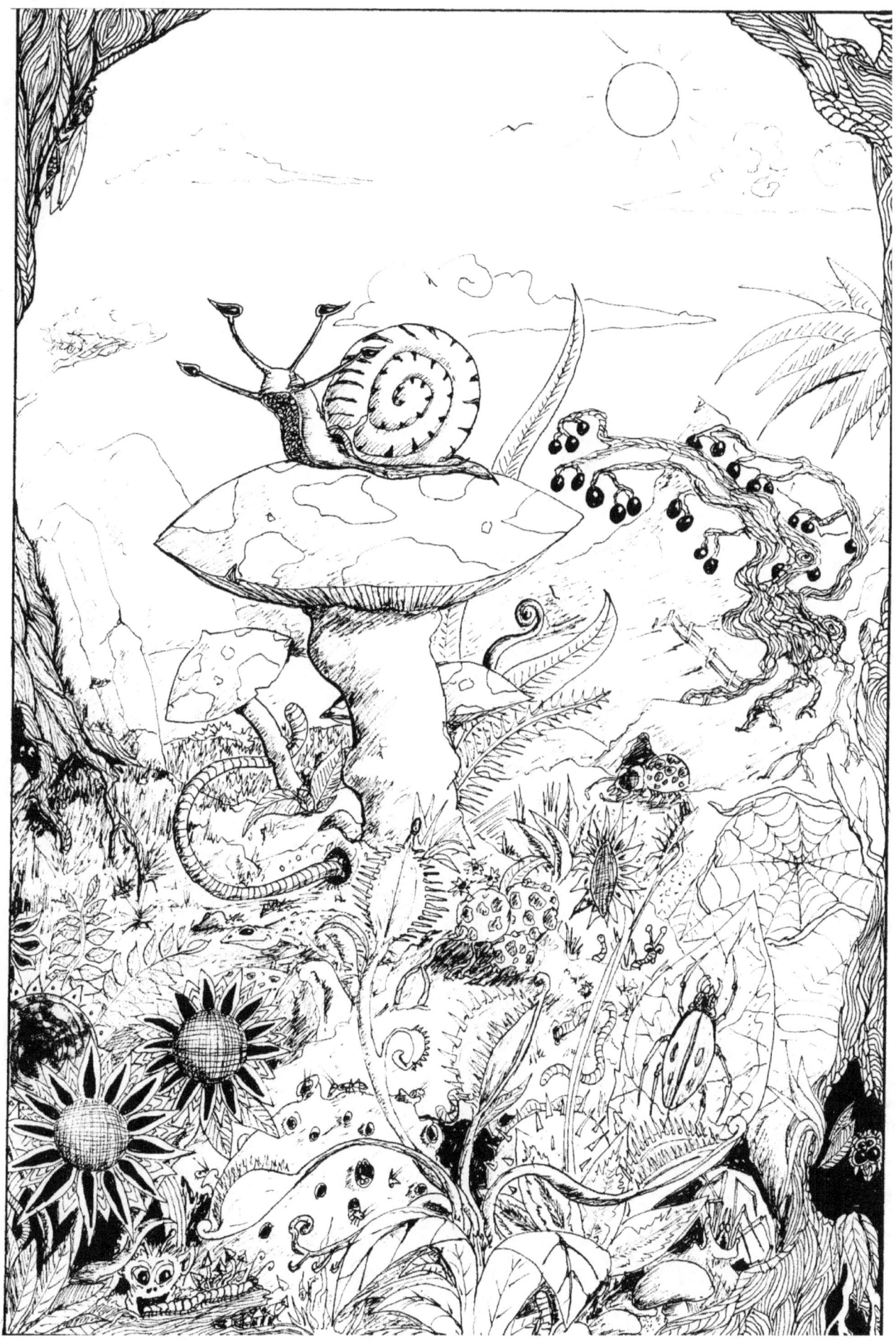

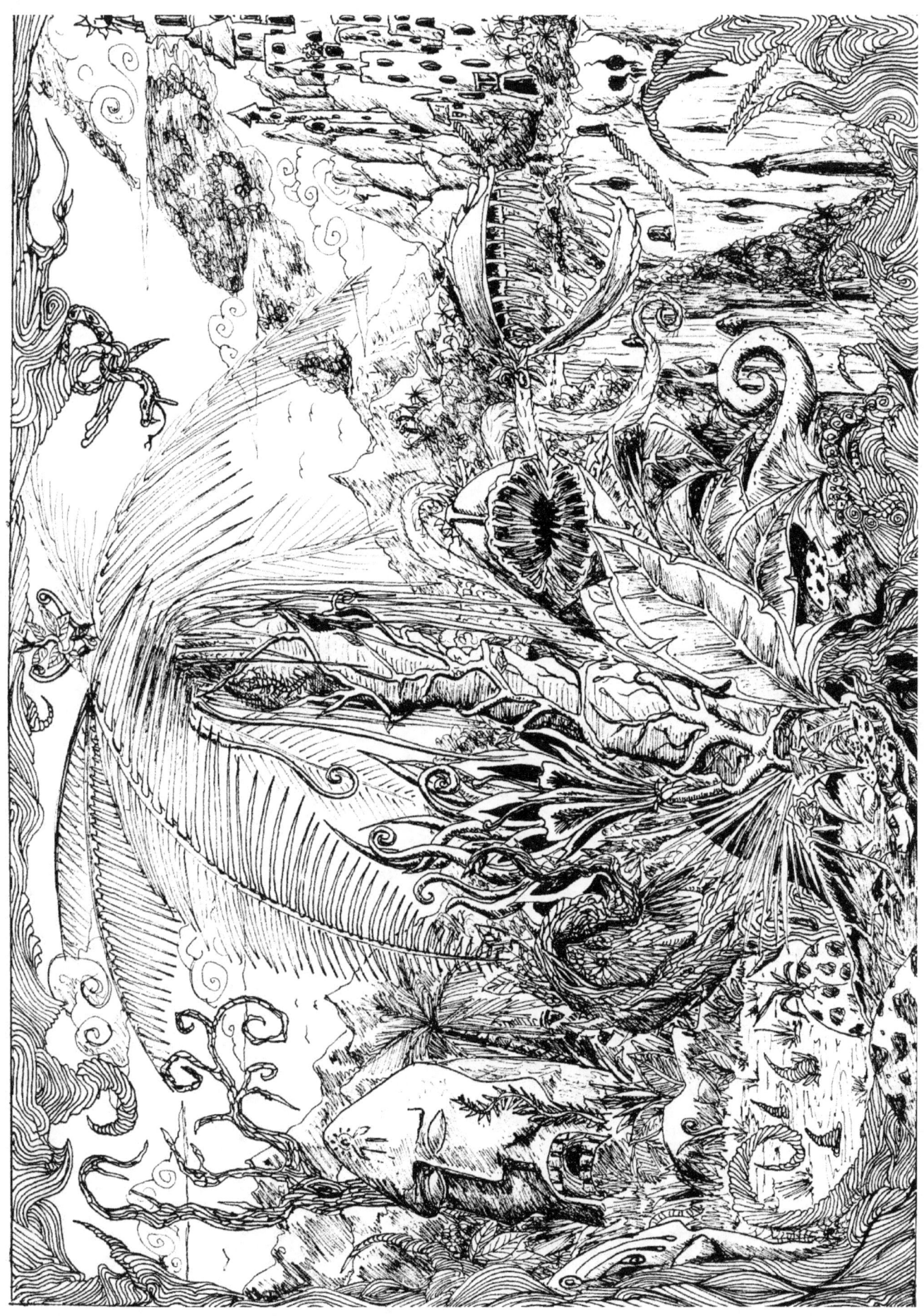

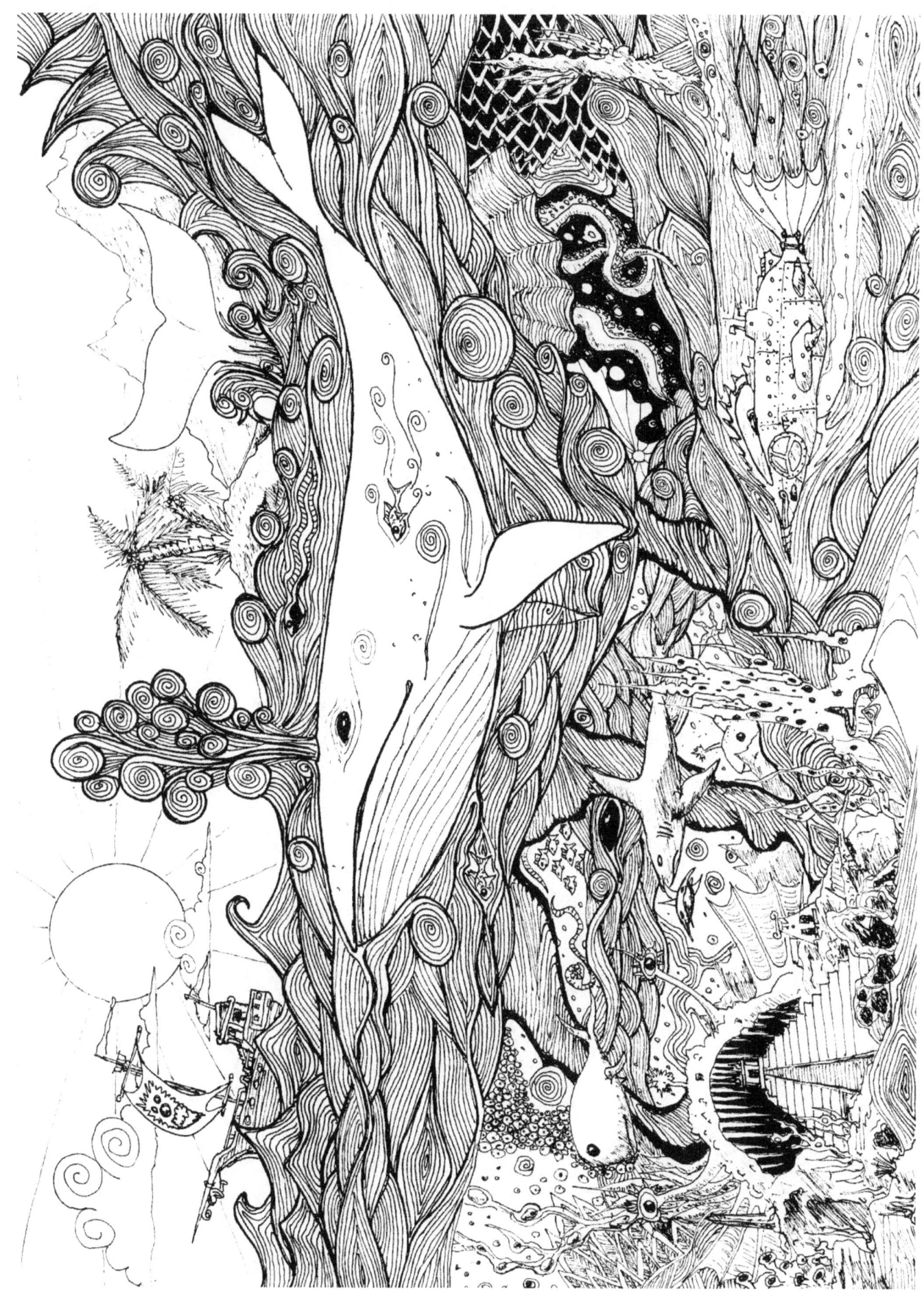

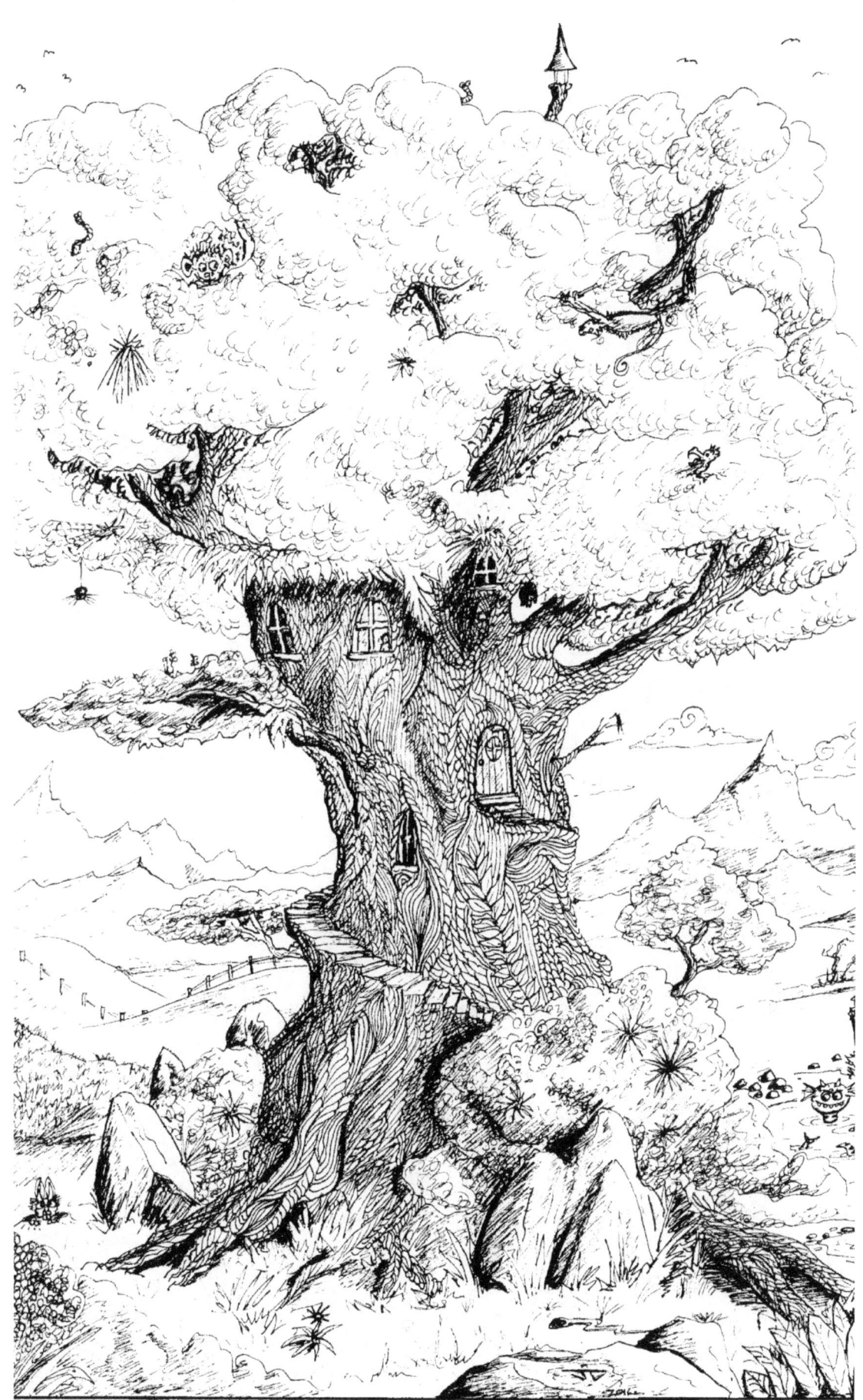

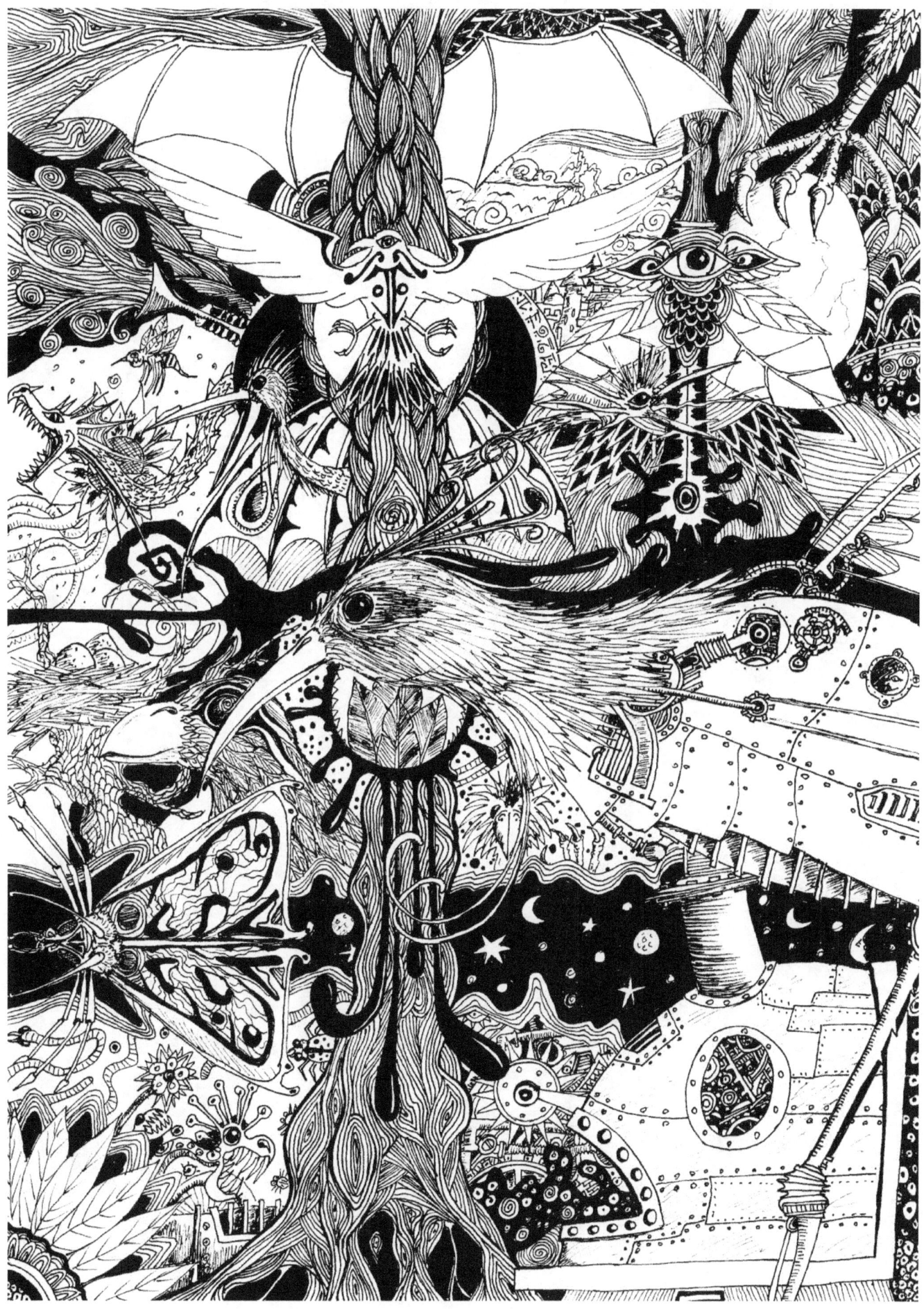

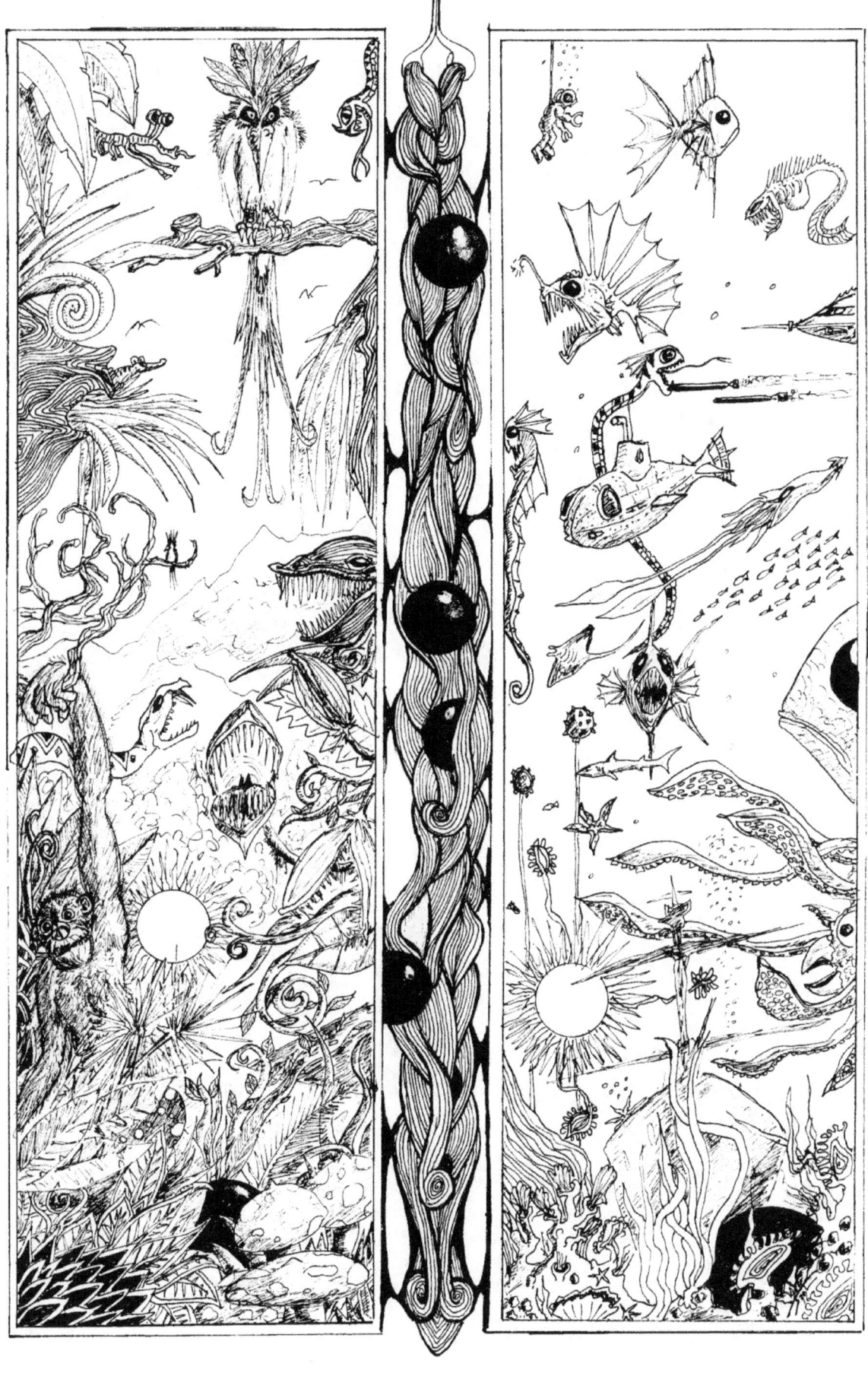

All Images Subject to Copyright © Joe Cowin 2016

www.ingramcontent.com/pod-product-compliance
Lightning Source LLC
Chambersburg PA
CBHW080614190526
45169CB00007B/3007